pocket guides

VISITING
CARD CASES

by

Noël Riley

Series Editor: Noël Riley

LUTTERWORTH PRESS
Guildford, Surrey

First published 1983

Cover illustration shows (*left to right, above*)
tortoiseshell concave-sided card case with inlaid
mother-of-pearl decoration; engraved and engine-turned
silver case by Edward Smith, Birmingham, 1858; and a
souvenir woodware case from Killarney in Ireland
(*below*) ivory case decorated with silver *piqué clouté*;
diamond-veneered case in two shades of mother-of-
pearl; and a mid-19th century press-moulded tortoiseshell
case showing a view of Abbotsford House.

ISBN 0–7188–2549–7

Printed in Great Britain by
Mackays of Chatham Ltd

Contents

1. A 'tablet' case by Samuel Davis, London, 1810. This is the earliest form of card case and probably contained an ivory tablet or *aide mémoire*.

Introduction

CARD cases – the slim rectangular holders of visiting cards made in many materials and countless styles from the 1820s for a century or more – are not just a reflection of a once important social habit. They provide a survey in microcosm of the techniques and artistic styles used for all kinds of objects during a hundred-year period. Card cases were made of silver and several other metals, mother-of-pearl, tortoiseshell, wood, lacquer, papier mâché, ivory, horn, leather and synthetic materials. Sometimes different materials and techniques were used in combination. Card cases were regarded, like the snuff boxes of an earlier period, as status-enhancing accessories, and they were nearly always finely made; their decoration, especially in examples designed for women, was often elaborate and complicated.

2. A silver envelope-shaped card case.

Like many fashionable habits, that of using calling cards was introduced by the French. By the end of the 18th century it had spread all over Europe, and by the beginning of the 19th it had developed into a highly complicated pattern of etiquette to which all ladies and gentlemen aspiring to the genteel ranks of society conscientiously conformed. Visiting cards were considered quite as efficacious as personal visits in maintaining polite contact between acquaintances.

Warne's *Etiquette for Gentlemen* (1866) spells out the calling system in detail:

'If your object is merely to drop cards, simply inquire after the health of the family and leave a card for the lady of the house. Where there are sisters or daughters, it is sometimes considered enough to turn down the corner of the card to intimate that they are included, but this is now rather going out. A separate card is now usually left for the young ladies, and one for the master of the house . . . three are sufficient to meet any case.' A married woman left her husband's card as well as her own. The author allowed that cards could be sent by a servant 'when a gentleman or a family are unexpectedly leaving town. In that case PPC (*pour prendre congé*) may be inserted in the corner.'

It was customary to leave cards rather than make personal calls on visits of condolence after a bereavement, and cards were also left the day after 'balls, receptions, private theatricals, amateur concerts and dinners'. If a gentleman caller found the lady of a house out he had to leave his card rather than visit her young daughters: 'Young ladies do not receive calls from gentlemen, unless they are very intimate with them or have passed the rubicon of thirty summers.'

The part played by visiting cards in the nuances of developing friendships is illustrated by an author of the 1830s: 'In the country, on a stranger taking possession of a house or estate, it is customary for such of the surrounding gentry who may desire his intimacy to call or leave their card. Such visits will of course be returned, if you are desirous of their connexion; if not, courtesy still demands a return card.' Although personal calls could not be made first by newcomers to a district, it was perfectly polite for them to leave cards with their established neighbours.

Visiting cards were probably derived from the habit of writing names on the backs of playing cards, and the earliest were about the same size. In the early 19th century, 'tablets' were used. These were the small ivory *aides mémoire* found in étuis and pocket books of the period. A caller would write his or her name on the tablet and have it conveyed by a servant to the person he or she was visiting. It would then be brought back to the caller with, presumably, a message of some sort (fig. 1). Individual cards must have been introduced during the 1820s and 30s and were of a more or less uniform size by the 1840s. Even then, a lady's card was generally larger than a gentleman's. Hers could be glazed, whereas a

3. An open-ended gentleman's case decorated with engraved foliage.

gentleman's should be 'small, thin and un-glazed . . . it should simply bear his name, preceded by Mr . . . there are occasions on which it is necessary for him to add his address in pencil and this is impractical on a glazed surface'. The names of daughters living at home were engraved below their mother's, 'in simple Italian writing, not Gothic or Roman letters, very small and without any flourishes'. Later, as well as the name and title of a lady or gentleman, his or her address was often engraved in the bottom corner. The popular portrait photographs on small cards known as *cartes de visite* were not, despite their name, generally used as visiting cards.

For carrying visiting cards a card case was usually considered 'neater and more con-venient than a pocket book'; while the habit by 'some barbarians' of using a pocket in a cigar case was dismissed as 'execrable' by the author of *Etiquette for Gentlemen* 'as the odour of tobacco is an offensive taint to many persons . . .' Pockets in cigar cases were definitely 'out' but some small hinged cases were made with separate divisions for a note-book, pencil and visiting cards.

However, most of the 19th century gentry, it seems, used cases designed for no other purpose than carrying cards. They were always basically rectangular but came in many outline shapes, from the straight or slightly convex sided to the curvaceous 'castle-topped' varieties. The usual dimensions were about three inches by four inches in the 1830s and 1840s and a little smaller in the next decades. Gentlemen's card cases, like their visiting cards, were customarily smaller than ladies' throughout the period. A favoured form during the late 19th century was the envelope shape, generally suspended on a chain with a ring for attaching it to a chatelaine (fig. 2). Corresponding with these, presumably ladies', card cases were the small, open-ended types usually shaped in a curve to fit a gentleman's pocket (fig. 3).

Opening mechanisms were equally varied. The most straightforward of all were those whose closely fitting lids simply slid on and off, and these were satisfactorily produced in most materials. However, the majority of cases

4. A group of card cases showing various methods of opening.

had hinged lids which opened sideways by pressing a small button. Other types included cases which opened out like books with concertina-like pockets for cards, spring-fitted lids which pop up when the side button is pressed and slip-top cases with spring-opening bottoms fitted with pockets (fig. 4). An 'automatic' card case, invented by Mark Freeman in 1843 was fitted with a press-button mechanism which opened the lid and delivered a single card at the same time. Variations on this theme appeared during the succeeding decades, but are rarely found in working order now. A late and rather elegant development was the swivelling card case which could be neatly tipped up to reveal its contents. This type dates from the early 20th century.

5. A silver card case made in Birmingham, 1897, with its original fitted leather outer case.

Most card cases have red velvet linings, now faded to a mellow pink; sometimes this velvet did not extend to the bottom of the case but merely covered an inch or two round the opening. Metal examples were often gilt inside. A few were carefully kept in leather outer cases, and where these have survived, the card cases are generally in pristine condition (fig. 5). An advertisement for the silversmithing firm of Mappin & Webb in a newspaper of 1894 included a 'Gentleman's Sterling Silver Card-Case, richly engraved £1.11s.6d Ditto Plain £1.7s. Complete in Morocco Case'.

The majority of all card cases has a small rectangular plate on one end or a cartouche on the front or back panel for the owner's name or initials. Many were never filled in, but occasionally a name remains, giving a card case an especially personal connection with the past.

1.   Silver

6. *(above)* An engraved view of the Chain Pier, Brighton, with engine-turning in the surrounding panels, by Nathaniel Mills, Birmingham, 1851.

S ILVER was probably the most widely used material for card cases. It was not only hard enough to provide protection for the cards within but sufficiently durable to withstand years of wear. It is significant that of all the card cases to survive, those made of silver are, generally speaking, in better condition than others. Besides, silver automatically evokes a certain richness, and this must have been a consideration among the status-conscious Victorians. From the 1830s onwards, the small-workers of Birmingham produced vast numbers of silver card cases in many shapes and with a range of decorative techniques that included filigree work and bright-cutting, repoussé and embossing, etching and engraving, engine-turning, die-stamping and casting (figs 6–16).

7. An engraved view of the Scott Memorial, a favourite subject among Birmingham card case makers.

8. *(above left)* A deeply incised design of roses against a background of engine-lining, by Alfred Taylor, Birmingham, 1853.

9. *(above centre)* Various methods of engraving are combined in a geometric and scrolled design by George Unite, Birmingham, 1872.

10. *(above right)* An elegantly simple engine-turned case by RT, Birmingham, 1875.

11. *(below left)* A view of Exeter Cathedral with engine-turned panels above and below, by David Pettifer, Birmingham, 1850.

12. *(below centre)* An embossed coursing scene, Birmingham, 1904.

13. *(below right)* An embossed and chased case with a view of St. Paul's Cathedral on one side by Nathaniel Mills, Birmingham, 1843.

Filigree was used for some of the earliest metal card cases. Many of them have slip tops but some, probably those made after about 1840, have sideways-opening hinged lids (figs. 17, 18 and 19). Filigree was exempt from hallmarking and it is therefore hard to trace most examples. However it is certain that several Birmingham makers produced filigree card cases, among them Nathaniel Mills, Samuel Pemberton, Edward Munslow and F. Allen, and A. D. Loewenstark of the Strand in London. The last two exhibited at the Great Exhibition of 1851. Filigree work was also imported from the Continent, notably from Spain and Italy. At the Great Exhibition, specimens of gold and silver filigree, including card cases, were shown by at least two manufacturers from Malta. The Chinese also exported silver filigree cases. These are generally recognizable as they have designs of dragons and other unmistakably oriental motifs. Many were of a later period than the European filigree cases, and some have the

14. *(left)* Westminster Abbey embossed in high relief by Edward Smith, Birmingham, 1849.

15. *(centre)* A view of the Crystal Palace by Hilliard & Thomason, Birmingham, 1850.

16. *(right)* An elaborately scrolled case with a view of Windsor Castle inscribed 'Royal Windsor', Birmingham, 1904.

17. *(left)* A shaped filigree case with raised decoration in the central panel.

18. *(centre)* A filigree card case, possibly by Nathaniel Mills of Birmingham.

19. *(right)* An unusually small silver filigree case.

sideways-opening hinged tops common to most card cases of the second half of the 19th century.

Birmingham, 'the toy shop of Europe' according to Edmund Burke, was the re-nowned centre of production for all kinds of small items of silver including snuff boxes, vinaigrettes, vesta cases and 'toys'. Card cases, in a similar category of small silver accessories, are frequently found to have the marks of specialists such as Nathaniel Mills, Taylor & Perry, Hilliard & Thomason, Frederick Marson and George Unite, all of whom hailed from Birmingham (*see* list on page 61). Several of these craftsmen repre-sented the second or third generation of their families to practise silversmithing.

John Taylor, of the Taylor & Perry partner-ship, was the younger brother of Joseph Taylor who had had a substantial business, with premises in London as well as Birming-ham, in the early 19th century. His trade card reveals an interesting facet of the toy-making trade. It reads 'J. Taylor, Working Gold and Silversmith, Jeweller, Tortoiseshell and Ivory

20. A late Victorian silver case from Birmingham embossed with an all-over design of plants and shells.

21. *(above left)* An etched design of scrolling plants within shaped panels, Birmingham, 1900.

22. *(above centre)* A high-quality case with a die-stamped view of Newstead Abbey on one side and Abbotsford on the other, by Taylor & Perry, Birmingham, 1836.

23. *(above right)* An embossed view of the Royal Exchange (with Windsor Castle on the other side) by Joseph Willmore, Birmingham, 1844.

24. *(below left)* A repoussé view of the Houses of Parliament with scrolling decoration surrounding it and on the back, by Nathaniel Mills, Birmingham, 1844.

25. *(below centre)* Holyrood House embossed and engraved by Frederick Marson, Birmingham, 1855.

26. *(below right)* An embossed view of Osborne House, Isle of Wight, by Alfred Taylor, Birmingham, 1858.

27. An embossed view of an unidentified church or college building in an unusual sideways position on a card case by A & S, Birmingham, 1858.

Box, Gilt and General Toy Manufacturer, 35 Newhall Street, Birmingham, and 2 Bouverie Street, Fleet Street, London.' Although his working life was over before the hey-day of the visiting card case, this reference to ivory and tortoiseshell box- and toy-making alongside silver may be a clue to the activities of other, later craftsmen. It is at least likely that ivory and tortoiseshell card cases with inlaid silver decoration were made by silversmiths (*see* page 61).

Vast numbers of silver card cases have topographical subjects and these are known as castle-tops. Favourites such as Windsor Castle, the Houses of Parliament, Westminster Abbey, Abbotsford House, Newstead Abbey, the Albert Memorial, Crystal Palace, the Scott Memorial and Birmingham Town Hall are repeated over and over again. As with the lids on all types of boxes, sporting scenes and other figurative subjects are found, but the majority of non-topographical card cases are decorated with flowers, foliage and abstract patterns.

A large proportion of silver card cases made in the second half of the 19th century were decorated with all-over patterns of scrolls and plants, with or without a central cartouche for the owner's name or initials. Some were embossed but most were engraved or

28. A silver case with scrolling decoration surrounding a view inscribed 'Nile Phile', Birmingham, 1904.

acid-etched, and nearly all had the sideways-opening hinged lid (figs. 20 and 21).

The earliest castle-tops have straight sides and squared-off corners, with the featured scene in a central rectangle surrounded by scrolling plant decoration which is occasionally pierced. A different view often appears on each side of a case. For example Byron's Newstead Abbey and Scott's Abbotsford House, Westminster Abbey and the Houses of Parliament, Windsor Castle and Kenilworth Castle may be paired in this way (figs. 22 and 23).

29. An embossed and crisply chased pattern of Prince of Wales' feathers, surrounded by flowers and foliage, by Frederick Marson, Birmingham, 1844.

From the 1840s onwards there is normally a scene only on one side and the back is decorated all over with scroll and foliate patterns. At the same time, the decoration surrounding the topographical subject on the front is shaped around it more closely and the building is often in a 'portrait' (up and down) rather than a 'landscape' format. The shapes of the cases themselves also grew more elaborate in the 1840s and 50s, with rococo

30. *(left)* The Duke of Wellington's statue by Matthew Coles Wyatt. The statue was placed on the arch at Hyde Park Corner in 1846 and removed to Aldershot in 1883. This unusual case was made by Edward Smith, Birmingham, 1850.

31. *(centre)* An 'aesthetic' card case by Hilliard & Thomason, Birmingham, 1881.

32. *(right)* An oriental-inspired case with embossed birds and hawthorn blossom.

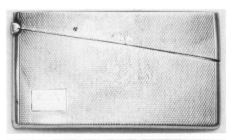

33. An engine-turned silver case shaped to fit a gentleman's pocket.

34. An embossed silver card case from America, *c.*1870.

scrolls and curlicues spilling into the outlines. Castle-tops were produced throughout the 19th century and into our own: those with the names of the scenes included are generally of very late 19th or early 20th century origin (figs. 24–30).

Around the 1880s the fashion for japonaiserie gave rise to card cases decorated in a distinctively oriental style, often with birds flying among bamboo shoots or hawthorn blossom; fan shapes, ferns and sunflowers are everywhere apparent (figs. 31 and 32). Some, more fanciful, had dragons and other oriental manifestations swirling over the surface. On the whole, the Japanese taste marked a return to simpler forms of decoration and a lightness of effect. Designs were engraved rather than embossed and did not always cover the whole surface of the silver. Sometimes gold wires or motifs such as flowers

35. An Indian silver card case of small proportions.

17

were applied or the design was parcel-gilt, but still the impression was one of restraint. Among the silversmiths who worked most successfully in the Japanese style were Barnard Brothers of London and Elkingtons of Birmingham.

Equally restrained and often beautifully made were the simple engine-turned cases which also stand out in elegant contrast to their busily patterned contemporaries of the 1870s and 1880s. Many have a central cartouche, and some were curved to fit a gentleman's pocket (fig. 33).

Some silver card cases were produced in America in the later years of the 19th century. Many are highly elaborate by comparison with English examples of the same period, and embossing in higher relief was customary. Complicated patterns of interlacing initials were among the Americans' favourite motifs for their more restrained examples. As American silver card cases are rarely hall-

36. *(left)* A gilt-metal card case with engraved decoration.

37. *(centre)* A silver-plated engraved case with black, blue and white enamel strapwork.

38. *(right)* A sideways-opening silver card case with applied scrolling decoration by JNM, London, 1891.

39. *(left)* An envelope card case by Sampson Mordan, London, 1907.

40. *(right)* A scroll-engraved case of envelope form.

marked properly, their origins are hard to trace, and they almost always fetch less money than their English silver counterparts (fig. 34).

The Indian silver cases which occasionally make their appearance on the market may have been produced for the English colonists in India who carried on their native habits with an intensity unrivalled at home. Most have hand-worked designs of plants or wild animals. Marked examples, like that impressed 'Dass & Dutt Calcutta' in the French Collection *(see* page 56) are unusual, but they are often of high quality and show an imaginative vigour (fig. 35).

At the upper end of the market, gold and silver-gilt card cases occasionally make their appearance. Less exotic are the brass and electroplated cases which are invariably decorated in imitation of silver (figs. 36, 37).

41. A Chinese export case with a pierced design of dragons amid clouds.

2.   Tortoiseshell

THE shell of the hawksbill turtle (*Eretmochelys imbricata*) to be found widely in the coastal waters of the tropics has been used for hundreds of years in decoration, and because of its fairly small size – an average adult shell is about 32 inches long – it has been an especially favoured embellishment for small boxes including card cases. Like other veneers the tortoiseshell plates were glued on to carcases of wood. Sometimes they were pressed with designs in relief and sometimes they were left smooth with silver or mother-of-pearl inlaid into them. In many the mottled figuring of the tortoiseshell by itself was most effective. Considerable numbers of card cases are found with carefully set panels of tortoiseshell divided by fine lines of pewter

42. *(left)* A mid-19th century mottled tortoiseshell case with inset ivory lines.

43. *(centre)* An early Victorian tortoiseshell case.

44. *(right)* A mid-19th century mottled tortoiseshell case with pewter lines inlaid on the surface.

or ivory. Some have no further embellishment except perhaps a small applied silver plate for the owner's initials (figs. 42–45).

However, tortoiseshell is a fairly pliable material, and can be moulded into shape by pressing under heat. Several card case makers exploited this. The Huguenot craftsman John Obrisset, who settled and worked in London in the early 18th century, had used heat pressing to make small tortoiseshell and horn boxes decorated with portraits in relief. Victorian craftsmen of the mid-19th century copied his technique for their figurative designs on the sides of card cases. These often took the form of views like Abbotsford House or Newstead Abbey surrounded by flowers and curlicues just like those on silver castle-tops, but more restrained architectural or floral motifs are also to be found (figs. 46 and 47).

Another revival of an earlier technique was

45. Mottled tortoiseshell bordered with mother-of-pearl.

46. *(left)* A press-moulded tortoiseshell case with a view of Abbotsford House on one side (and Newstead Abbey on the other), similar to silver castle-top designs (compare fig. 107).

47. *(right)* A press-moulded architectural design on a mid-19th century tortoiseshell case.

48. A tortoiseshell case with a vermicular pattern in *piqué d'or* (or *piqué clouté*).

the fine inlaying of gold or silver studs and strips into a tortoiseshell or ivory background, known as piqué work. It had been developed by a 17th century Neapolitan jeweller named Laurentini, and was adopted enthusiastically by craftsmen in Paris and London during the 18th century. Their finely decorated snuff boxes, étuis and other objects of vertu are now much sought-after by collectors. Late in the 18th century, Matthew Boulton adapted piqué work to factory methods, and card case makers later used his technique for inlaying designs of silver into tortoiseshell and ivory. Some piqué card cases, however, were made by hand in the mid-19th century.

Piqué work was basically of two kinds: *piqué d'or* (also known as *piqué clouté*) in which tiny pinheads or points were inlaid in patterns on the tortoiseshell or ivory surface (fig. 48), and *piqué posé*, whereby designs were cut in thin sheets of silver and inlaid into the heated

49. A tortoiseshell case inlaid with silver *piqué posé* in a design showing the oriental influence of the 1880s.

surface of the tortoiseshell. When it cooled the tortoiseshell contracted and held the metal fast. This was then finished with hand-chasing and the whole surface burnished and polished. *Piqué posé* was used most often for inlaying silver into tortoiseshell (fig. 49). The technique was less satisfactory for inlaying ivory and is rarely found. *Piqué clouté* with either gold or silver pinheads and sometimes a mixture of the two, was used with great success on both ivory and tortoiseshell cases. Those decorated in this way are among the most beautiful of all.

The contrasting tones of tortoiseshell and silver *piqué posé* were successfully exploited in the 1880s, by makers – presumably silver-smiths, though their work is rarely marked – working in the Aesthetic style. One of them, Sampson Mordan, is thought to have had a commercial agreement with the publishers (Routledge) of Kate Greenaway's books and

50. A tortoiseshell case inlaid with a silver Kate Greenaway design, probably by Sampson Mordan.

many of his small silver wares were engraved with children and mob-capped figures in her idiom. Occasionally he used tortoiseshell as a background for silver Kate Greenaway motifs (fig. 50).

Mother-of-pearl was inlaid into tortoise-shell in a similar way, though the technique should not be called piqué work. In these cases, designs were predominantly natural-istic, with birds, flowers and foliage gleaming in delicate contrast to the brownish tortoise-shell background. To make them, tiny frag-ments of shell were cemented into the tortoiseshell surface and the whole was then polished to a uniform smoothness (figs. 51–54). It is extremely rare to find ivory designs inlaid into tortoiseshell on card cases, almost certainly because of the technical problems involved.

Some card cases of Indian origin combine tortoiseshell and ivory decoration over a sandalwood core. In these, the tortoiseshell is used as the background and bands of carved and incised ivory form an applied strapwork over the surface. This is sometimes highly elaborate, with tiny balls of ivory forming rather bumpy highlights, and is a far cry from the delicate tortoiseshell cases with gold piqué decoration produced in England (fig. 55).

Another type of tortoiseshell case produced

51. *(above left)* A concave-sided tortoiseshell case with mother-of-pearl inlays.

52. *(above right)* Mother-of-pearl flowers and stars inlaid into a tortoiseshell case of the 1840s. The stems of the flowers are of finely twisted silver wire.

53. *(below left)* Incised and inlaid mother-of-pearl flowers inlaid in a gentleman's tortoiseshell card case.

54. *(below right)* A mother-of-pearl flower spray on a small (probably man's) tortoiseshell case.

55. A tortoiseshell veneered case overlaid with ivory arabesques, typical of Indian work.

in England had gem-painted panels. This was a type of painting behind glass which had been pioneered by a Miss Tonge of Boston in Lincolnshire in the 1840s. Painted views of favourite tourist haunts such as Shakespeare's House, Westminster Abbey, 'The New Houses of Parliament', St Paul's Cathedral and miscellaneous castles are found. They were often backed with metallic foil or with pearl shell; this type was known as 'patent pearl glass'. The paintings were set into tortoiseshell and also papier mâché card cases of the 1850s. Some were exhibited at the Great Exhibition by T. Lane of Birmingham who had patented pearl glass in papier mâché in 1849.

Carved tortoiseshell cases are occasionally found, and these are nearly always of oriental – probably Chinese – origin. They are not usually carved all over like the Chinese carved horn cases (with which they should not be

56. A swivelling tortoiseshell card case of small dimensions, probably dating from the 1920s.

confused – they are much lighter in weight) but have their smooth polished surfaces relieved by elaborate carving in borders and cartouches on both sides. In these cases – which are rare – the tortoiseshell is exceptionally thick and is used in the solid rather than veneered on to a wood carcase. Some immaculate tortoiseshell card cases were produced in Japan in the late 19th century. Again, they were not veneered but were made of solid tortoiseshell and decorated in the *shibayama* technique with plant sprays, insects, birds and so on, in gold and colours.

Later, in England, thin plates of tortoiseshell were used most stylishly for card cases which swivelled within narrow frames. This way of using tortoiseshell on its own, rather than as a veneer on a wooden carcase, and without any surface decoration, gave it a lustrous transparency entirely in keeping with the art deco style (fig. 56).

3.   Ivory

57. An ivory card case of the 1830s decorated with a flower spray in silver *piqué clouté*.

I VORY was used successfully for both carved and inlaid card cases. During the 1830s and 1840s most ivory examples were decorated with piqué point inlay, and these are some of the most attractive of all. They generally have the sideways-opening hinged lid and press-button clip common to a large proportion of silver cases and most of those made of tortoiseshell, mother-of-pearl and papier-mâché. The tiny metallic studs – both silver and gold were used – were arranged in repeating patterns or in simple floral designs, and they have a restrained delicacy which is not found in later examples. The pins used in *piqué clouté* – the term comes from the French word, *clou*, for nail – varied in size and the point decoration was sometimes used with incised lines or whorls to accentuate the patterns (figs. 57, 58 and cover).

By about the 1850s piqué of this type had

58. An ivory case decorated with silver *piqué clouté* and carved whorls.

59. A rounded design reminiscent of quilting on an ivory case of the mid-19th century.

60. A polished ivory case of the 1850s with applied silver decoration.

given way to a much more sumptuous use of ivory. Card cases were rounded instead of squared off at the edges and either decorated with applied silver mounts or carved with curvaceous, cushiony designs reminiscent of the period's upholstery. These effects were heightened by the satin-like gloss to which the surfaces were polished (figs. 59, 60).

A large proportion of the carved ivory examples to be found nowadays were the work of Chinese craftsmen working for the European market. Their fanciful designs of figures and flowers, trees and pagodas, are repeated in many materials – ivory, horn, wood and coromandel lacquer. Many of these 'Chinese export' cases are covered on all sides with a profusion of carving; others have smoothly polished panels with carved reserves. The quality varies greatly: some are extremely finely carved whether in high or low relief

60a. Detail showing the unusual book form of fig. 60. The pencil slides into slots on each leaf to keep the case closed.

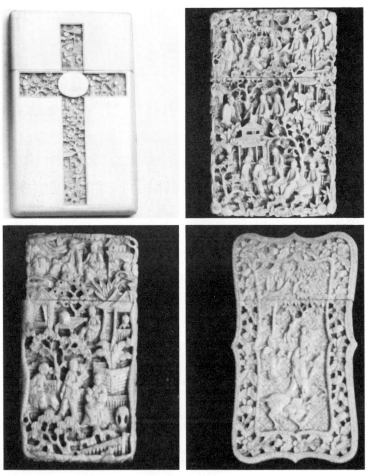

61. *(above left)* A Chinese carved ivory case made for export.

62. *(above right)* A vigorously carved Chinese ivory card case.

63. *(below left)* A Chinese ivory card case carved with a typical figurative scene, but of unusually small proportions.

64. *(below right)* Another Chinese case carved in shallow relief with figures and plants within a shaped border of flowers and leaves.

65. A Japanese ivory case with gilded and mother-of-pearl decoration in the relief technique known as *shibayama*.

while others are comparatively coarse. Among the best and certainly the most restrained examples are those with life-like fruits carved and then stained on the polished ivory surface, but these are rare compared with the lively figure subjects which seem to have been the usual Chinese export fare. But even among these, carving of the utmost delicacy and sharpness of detail can be found by the discerning. Invariably the lids of Chinese carved cases slide on and off with perfect precision over a bezel (figs. 61–64).

From Japan, late in the 19th century, come some outstanding ivory card cases with *shibayama* decoration. This may include butterflies, birds, insects and plants in horn, tortoiseshell, mother-of-pearl, jade, amber and other semi-precious materials. Less spectacular, but still of superb quality are the Japanese card cases of polished ivory with gold naturalistic decoration in relief (fig. 65).

India, land of the elephant, produced many

31

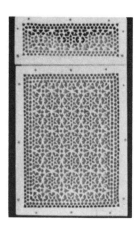

66. An Indian ivory case with carved and pierced filigree decoration.

different types of ivory card cases. Those decorated with tortoiseshell and ivory strapwork have already been mentioned. Some are covered with chequerboard patterns of the two materials and others again are of porcupine quillwork bordered with pierced ivory and carved bobbles. Of greater delicacy are those of carved and pierced ivory, usually in repeating patterns of rosettes and star like motifs. They are similar in shape and basic design to the Chinese export cases: like them the Indian examples have closely fitting slip tops, but unlike them their sides are generally rounded rather than squared and their carving is in shallower relief, giving them an altogether softer appearance (fig. 66). Less restrained are the Indian ivory card cases covered in a profusion of crisply carved flowers. These, which generally open book-fashion to reveal silk lined pockets for visiting cards, probably date from the later years of the 19th century.

Another type of ivory card case from India

67. Incised and blackened decoration on an unusual solid ivory case from India.

32

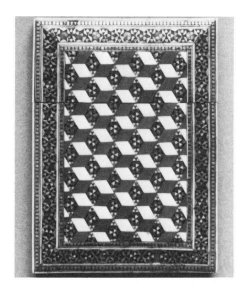

68. An Indian case with a
mosaic design in ivory,
sandalwood, ebony, mother-
of-pearl and pewter.

makes use of the incised and then blackened
surface decoration traditionally associated
with Vizagapatam and for many years a
valued European import. The cases themselves were generally of sandalwood or ebony
with ivory borders incised with patterns of
trailing plants and flowers (fig. 67). This incised ivory decoration is also found on the
mosaic work imported to Europe from India
from the 1880s onwards and sold in such
fashionable emporiums as Liberty's. Small
writing desks, caskets and boxes including
card cases were made of sandalwood covered
with star-like geometric patterns and borders.
These were made up from tiny fragments of
ivory, ebony and metal. Sometimes green-
stained ivory as well as white was used to give
a more colourful design. The mosaic patterns
were often surrounded by incised ivory
borders. In other cases the mosaic work
formed borders round a plain sandalwood
panel (fig. 68).

4.   Mother-of-pearl

MOTHER-OF-PEARL comes from the inside surfaces of oysters and various other molluscs, especially those found in the waters of Australasia and the south Pacific. The shell was used for card cases in a similar way to tortoiseshell, generally in the form of veneers glued to wooden bases. However, because the slices of shell were usually much smaller than tortoise-shell plates, they were rarely used in sheet-like veneers, but were cut into diamond shapes to create an attractive patchwork effect. These diamonds were sometimes divided by metal strips which provided an effectively dark foil for the light iridescence of the shell (figs. 69–71). In many cases the surface of the pearl

69. A mother-of-pearl case of the mid-19th century with its diamond-shaped veneers interspersed with fine metal strips.

70. *(left)* An unusual design of mother-of-pearl with metal strips.

71. *(right)* A diamond veneered mother-of-pearl case with a shaped outline.

itself was engraved with patterns (fig. 72). In others, a decorative effect was produced by combining the usual pale whitish shell with darker greenish blue. This was either set in interspersing diamonds on the front and back surfaces or laid as borders round the other panels (figs. 73–75). Very rarely, one finds a mother-of-pearl card case with a shaped outline and relief embellishment not unlike a silver castle-top but with a central figurative rather than topographical design (fig. 77).

Mother-of-pearl card cases probably form the majority of those not made of silver and were produced in vast numbers in the 1840s and 1850s. Although the variety of techniques for making them is limited in comparison with other materials, they succeed in providing enormous differences in the detail of their patterning as well as the quality with which they were originally made. It is a pity that the names of more makers of tortoiseshell, ivory

72. An engraved mother-of-pearl case.

73. *(above left)* Diamonds of white pearl shell interspersed with dark blue-green on a mid-19th century example.

74. *(above right)* Fine strips of dark shell frame the light-coloured geometric decoration on a case which opens book-wise. The central lozenge bearing the owner's monogram is of engraved silver.

75. *(below left)* Another combination of light and dark shell in an unusual arrangement of strips.

76. *(below right)* A fine marquetry of mother-of-pearl and twisted silver wire (for the flower stems) inlaid into tortoiseshell with light and dark pearl shell in the surrounding sections.

77. A rare mother-of-pearl case with a shaped outline and a central panel of Japanese *shibayama* decoration.

and mother-of-pearl card cases are not known: there must have been a great many working around the middle years of the 19th century in Birmingham where the pearl button trade was centred.

Among the exhibitors at the Great Exhibition in 1851, however, Richard Peters and Son of Birmingham showed 'card cases in various coloured pearls and tortoiseshell, of new designs and patterns . . . lady's card case in two coloured pearls, consisting of 730 distinct pieces of diamond-shaped shell . . . card case, novel shape, in tortoiseshell, studded with silver, with painting in the centre.' Other manufacturers of items in mother-of-pearl and tortoiseshell included H. Chatwin and John Hayden, both of Birmingham, and card cases may well have been among their exhibits.

5. Papier mâché

PAPIER MÂCHÉ was one of the most widespread decorative materials of the early Victorian period. The lustrous black background with colourful painting, gilded highlights and pearl inlays that were characteristic of the papier mâché produced in the 1840s and 1850s exuded the solid opulence so beloved of the Victorians. Developed in the late 18th century by Henry Clay who exploited it most successfully in the making of trays, the material was later used for all manner of articles from chairs and tables – even beds – to tea caddies, inkstands and writing equipment, small baskets and coasters, handscreens, clock cases and boxes of all kinds. Card cases were inevitably among

78. A black papier mâché case with inlaid pearl decoration and gilded embellishments.

these. It has been said that papier mâché card cases were made as early as 1826; they were certainly being produced in large quantities by the japanners of Birmingham and Wolverhampton by the early 1840s.

From the firm of McCallum & Hodson of Birmingham we have a record of their method of making card cases in the mid-19th century, and it is likely that other firms used a similar technique. Long narrow pieces of greased wood were covered on both sides with layers of pasted paper. When sufficient layers had been added the entire length was immersed in linseed oil for five or ten minutes to amalgamate the paper into one mass. The whole was then stove-dried and the wood removed, leaving a papier mâché tube. This was then cut into card case lengths and the ends added.

Nearly all papier mâché card cases have sideways-opening hinged lids and press-

79. Fragments of pearl shell inlaid into black papier mâché in a flower vase design. The opening edges of this case, like many other papier mâché examples, are banded with ivory.

39

button fastenings, and the opening edges are often finished with neat bands of ivory (figs. 78, 79). In form, most are of the straight-sided rectangular variety, but some of the later examples are convex (fig. 80). More rare and exciting than almost any others are the shaped-sided cases with finely painted scenes on the fronts and backs. These were probably produced by the firm of Spiers of Oxford, dealers in all kinds of fancy goods and well known for their papier mâché souvenirs. It is likely that they bought articles 'in the blank' that is, undecorated, from other firms such as Alsager & Neville of Birmingham, and undertook the painting themselves. Their subjects were often views and buildings in Oxford, painted with exceptional fineness (fig. 81).

Birmingham and Wolverhampton were the main centres of production and the Birmingham firm of Jennens & Bettridge was

80. A convex case with 'Renaissance' decoration in pearl, colours and gilding.

81. A shaped papier mâché case painted with an Oxford view and probably sold by Spiers.

undoubtedly the best known producer of papier mâché. The business successor to Henry Clay, the firm became papier mâché manufacturer to Queen Victoria. Jennens & Bettridge had showrooms in London, and in New York in 1851–52, and continued in business in Birmingham until 1867. They employed some of the best decorators of the period and, to ensure the highest standards, employed outside instructors to teach painting in the factory. The result was a range of wares painted with outstanding skill and subtlety. Flowers painted 'on the black' were always among the favourite subjects, but exotic birds came a close second. Gold highlights and borders were used liberally and some artists made use of gold and bronze powders in their polychrome compositions, or added metallic 'speckling' to the backgrounds (fig. 82).

Jennens & Bettridge took out patents for several decorating techniques including a method of pearl shell inlay, but other makers, among them McCallum & Hodson, Footherape Showell & Shenton, and Richard Turley, all of Birmingham, used mother-of-pearl to decorate papier mâché. Thin slips of shell were glued to the surface of an object and the surrounding ground was then built up with varnish till the whole area was satiny smooth. Painted details were filled in before the final sealing coats of varnish were applied. The technique was used a great deal for decorating card cases, generally with posies of flowers whose petals and leaves were of pearl shell (figs. 78, 83).

A slightly later development was the use of pearl shell inlays to simulate jewels on the surfaces of objects. Gold leaf was used to create garland-like patterns and rich bands studded with painted and pearl-inlaid baubles in pseudo-Renaissance style (fig. 80). Similar were the 'Persian' decorations in which arabesques and strapwork patterns in white and bright colours were outlined in gold. These were popular in the 1860s and 70s (fig. 84).

Other types of papier mâché decoration used for card cases included simulated

82. *(left)* An exotically painted papier mâché case with bronze speckling in the background and gilded rococo decoration.

83. *(right)* A black papier mâché case with inlaid leaves of mother-of-pearl, and painted decoration in gold, red, green and yellow.

84. *(left)* A 'Persian' design painted in gold, yellow, red, blue and green on a black papier mâché ground.

85. *(right)* A gem-painted panel of St Paul's Cathedral with a painted strapwork border. Gem paintings were used on tortoiseshell as well as papier mâché card cases in the mid-19th century.

tortoiseshell and marbling, generally with gold curlicues and trailing patterns. Gem-painted panels were used in a similar way to those on tortoiseshell cases, but with colourfully painted frames on the black papier mâché grounds (fig. 85). The backs of these cases were often left plain. The names of George Davies and T. Lane, both of Birmingham, are linked with the production of gem-painted papier mâché cases.

6. Leather

SOME of the earliest card cases were of leather. One, in the French collection at the Harris Museum, Preston, is a small slip-top case in brown leather with 'Elizabeth Chapman September 26 1821' inscribed in ink on the bezel. Others, of red, green or brown leather, had tooled decoration like bookbindings but were of the same simple design and were probably made in the 1820s. Thomas Best, a maker of red leather jewel caskets, miniature chests of drawers and other small boxes, is known to have produced card cases of this type. Sometimes leather formed a framework for needlework panels in fine silk cross-stitch on the sides of card cases. These were almost certainly worked by ladies and given away as keepsakes.

86. A tooled leather case of the 1850s or 60s.

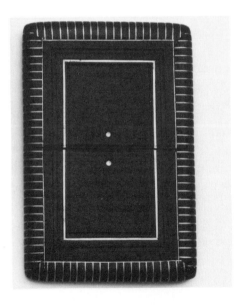

87. Another tooled leather card case showing the way the split sides open on a spring to reveal the card compartments when the lid is pulled off.

Opening mechanisms and interior fittings of card cases can be seen in enormous variety in those made of leather. The simple slide-off lid was most usual until about 1835 or 40, after which time the hinge-top seems to have been used as often. Later in the century other variations of the slip-top theme appeared. In one of these the bottom or main part of the case was split-sided and fitted with a simple spring mechanism which popped open when the lid was taken off to show several card compartments within. Their sombre leather outsides, often tooled in gold, and contrasting silk linings in brilliant shades of blue or green, make these cases strikingly elegant (figs. 86, 87).

Some more subdued cases in black leather were produced for mourning. Although they generally open sideways across the top quarter of the case like so many others, they sometimes have three compartments inside: two for the husband's and wife's visiting cards and a third for a pencil (fig. 88).

45

88. A black leather
mourning card case.

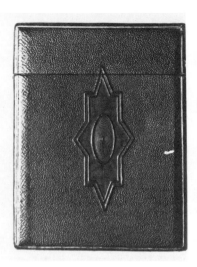

A few card cases, especially high quality
examples in gold or silver, were sold in pro-
tective leather boxes which have helped to
preserve them in perfect condition. Many of
these 'card case cases' were themselves carefully made with tooled designs and ingenious
fastenings. As some inevitably have become
separated from their original contents and
their purpose is not always obvious to the
uninitiated, they are well worth looking out
for. Sometimes they may be confused with the
photographic cases of the period, or with
cheroot cases, but their proportions should be
unmistakable to a well-seasoned card case
collector.

Among the known makers of leather card
cases are De La Rue who exhibited 'pocket-
books, wallets and card-cases, in leather and
velvet' among their stationery wares at the
Great Exhibition of 1851, and Thomas Best of
Birmingham, already mentioned, who made
both ladies' and gentlemen's card cases
among other leather goods.

7.   Wood

A REPRESENTATIVE collection of wooden card cases would encompass a high proportion of the many decorative methods used for wood wares of all kinds during the 19th century. As well as straightforward carved or painted wood used in the solid, there were veneered forms and more specialized kinds of surface decoration such as penwork, Tunbridge mosaic, Killarney work or Mauchline ware. Furthermore, card cases made of wood are among the least expensive: interesting purchases can still be made in the £10–£20 bracket.

Some of the earliest wooden card cases were decorated with penwork, a form of painting developed, largely as an amateur pastime, to imitate ivory inlay. Designs, which generally

89. A penwork case with a typical chinoiserie subject, probably dating from the 1840s.

90. A Tunbridge miniature mosaic landscape in a rococo style surround on a mid-19th century card case.

91. An English parquetry card case.

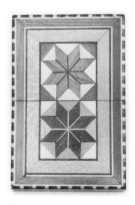

took the form of chinoiserie scenes, were 'voided' on to black backgrounds and details worked up in a pen-and-ink technique. Sometimes colours like red and green, or even gold, were used for highlights. Penwork card cases are comparatively rare but they have a naïve charm which is especially endearing. No two are alike, and most were painted by amateurs, as keepsakes, around the 1840–1850 period (fig. 89).

Many of the wooden card cases made in Europe were of various kinds of souvenir woodware. Tunbridge is the best known of these, and card cases are occasionally found decorated with the minute wood mosaic designs which had been famous since the 18th century. In this technique square hardwood sticks about the size of matches, of differing coloured woods, were glued together to form a picture or pattern. When dry, thin slices of the design could be sawn off and glued to the tops

92. Another parquetry
design on an English
mid-19th century case.

of boxes and other objects to form mosaic-
like decoration. Edmund Nye, a well-known
Tunbridge maker, is thought to have produced card cases of this type among his other
wares (fig. 90).

Parquetry, that is, geometrical veneers of
various coloured woods, was also used for card
cases. Patterns were made from triangular,
square, rectangular and diamond-shaped
slices of wood of different shades, interspersed
with contrasting bands. Unlike Tunbridge
mosaic ware, in which the end-grain of the
wood forms the pattern, this type of decoration
makes use of the side-grain laid in different
directions to enhance the effect of the varying
kinds and colours of wood. Some of these
abstract patterned parquetry card cases were
produced in and around Tunbridge Wells, but
a similar type of parquetry ware was also
imported from Sorrento in Italy. The use of
woods dyed to shades of green, red and blue

93. *(left)* A typical tartan ware card case of the late 19th century.

94. *(right)* A Killarney work case from Ireland.

as well as natural-coloured distinguishes Sorrento wares from the true Tunbridge examples (figs. 91, 92).

The brightly coloured tartan wares made from the 1830s at Laurencekirk by Charles Stiven and at Mauchline by the Smith brothers, and later also by other Scottish makers, included many card cases. In the earliest examples the patterns were painted directly on to the wood (generally sycamore) but from mid-century they were printed on paper which was then glued to the surface and varnished. They were still being produced at the turn of this century (fig. 93).

Of similar Scottish origin are the light-coloured sycamore boxes decorated with transfer-printed views of famous buildings and beauty spots all over the British Isles. Card cases in this type of ware seem to be less common than those in the lustrous tartan ware. One in the French collection has a vignette of the Pass of Killiecrankie and is marked 'Dunkeld McLean & Son Publishers'. Others were made 'from wood on the estate' of such places as Abbotsford or Drumlanrig and are decorated with views of them.

Another form of souvenir wood-ware in which card cases can be found occasionally is Killarney work, a cottage industry apparently started, like others in Ireland, to bring relief to the poor. Naïve views of subjects like Killarney Castle, or simple sprigs of shamrock were scored in light-coloured wood panels with a red hot needle. Contrastingly dark woods like yew or bog oak were used as decorative surrounds, or mosaic patterns were introduced. The cases were often made to simulate books, complete with tooled bindings, and they have a unique form of opening in which a small section at the top of the spine slides out like a pencil box top. Nearly all have 'Killarney Lakes' rather unevenly inscribed in silvered pokerwork (fig. 94). At the Great Exhibition, Dennis Connell of Dublin, 'carver

95. A Chinese export carved wood case with a typical figurative subject.

96. A painted wood case of another type of oriental export ware.

and producer', showed 'Bookstands, chess-boards, card-cases etc from arbutus wood [from the strawberry tree, a type of evergreen] grown at the lakes of Killarney.'

The carved Chinese export cases are instantly recognizable but although the subject matter and style varied little from one material to another, the wooden examples are generally crude by comparison with their counterparts in lacquer, ivory or horn (fig. 95). The wood most often used was sandal-wood, but boxwood and much heavier ebony examples can be found. Carved sandalwood or ebony cases were also made in India. These were not decorated with the conversation subjects typical of the Chinese but most often with stylized flowers and borders similar to Indian ivory carvings.

Of distinctly subtle hue were the painted cases, generally depicting tranquil landscapes or boating scenes with trees and mountains, which were also exported from the East in the second half of the 19th century. Highlights were often in low relief and the background colours were dark blues or metallic greys (fig. 96).

8.   Miscellaneous Materials

AS we have seen, Japan produced some spectacular card cases of ivory or tortoiseshell decorated in the *shibayama* technique with incrustations of ivory, tortoise-shell, coral, mother-of-pearl or semi-precious stones. *Shibayama* was also applied to lacquer and from time to time Japanese lacquer card cases with this type of decoration are to be found. More often lacquer card cases decorated in relief (*Takamaki-e*), or colours with or without gold decoration are dis-covered by lucky collectors. These were export pieces – the card case as we know it was not a Japanese accessory – and they were made with exquisite artistry. Like other, essentially Japanese, boxes they have no hinges or catches and the lids slide on and off with velvet precision.

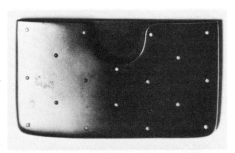

97. A Japanese gun-metal gentleman's case inlaid with turquoise.

98. A Japanese gun-metal case with a colourful design of cock, hen and chicken.

99. A rare example in black
sealing wax.

Among other Japanese exports, more rare
but less exotic, were card cases made of gun
metal. They were generally inlaid with semi-
precious materials or enamelled. The grey
metal with which they were made gives them a
somewhat sombre appearance, and their
small size (often curved to fit a pocket) pro-
claims them to have been intended for gentlemen's visiting cards (figs. 97, 98). Chinese
exports included carved horn card cases
similar to those of ivory and wood already dis-
cussed. Some are of higher quality than others
but they vary little in subject matter.

Brilliantly colourful *cloisonné* enamel card
cases, sometimes studded with jewels, were
mostly produced in Russia late in the 19th and
early this century. The Russian jeweller Carl
Fabergé is also known to have made card cases
in his own inimitably rich style.

Shagreen or sharkskin was a favoured
material for all kinds of cases in the 18th
century, but its use had virtually died out by

the Victorian period and a shagreen card case must have been a rarity. At least one example has been found, however. It was of the sideways opening hinged top variety and straight rectangular shape typical of the 1830s or 40s and the delicacy of its pale green colouring was enhanced by ivory edging bands.

The mouldable properties of sealing wax must have seemed attractive indeed in an age when plastics were still undeveloped. In the Great Exhibition several manufacturers apparently exhibited sealing waxes of various kinds, 'with impressions'. One of them, Hyde and Co., showed 'a new mode of taking impressions from stone, metal and composition intaglios'. Perhaps he inspired the outlandish sealing wax card case with its moulded medallions, almost certainly made as a mourning accessory (fig. 99).

100. An exceedingly fine silver card case inset with cameo views of Rome, possibly a special commission.

Tips on Collecting:
what to pay and what to look for

101. A silver case embossed on one side with a view of the Scott Memorial, otherwise chased with scrolls and plants. It was made by Nathaniel Mills, Birmingham, 1844, which accounts for the high price it reached (£200) at Bonhams in 1981.

ALTHOUGH many museums have small selections of card cases, none can rival the French collection at the Harris Museum, Preston. It consists of more than 900 examples, collected over a period of 30 or 40 years by Mrs C. A. L. French who eventually gave it to the Museum. Sample groups are on permanent display in the galleries, but the whole collection is available for study by appointment with the Keeper of Decorative Arts. It is well worth a special journey.

One of the delights of collecting card cases is the fact that they can turn up anywhere. Their haunts are as diverse as the cases themselves, and range from exclusive jewellers' establishments to the local junk market. Similarly their prices vary enormously. The most expensive, in gold, or rare examples by highly regarded makers like Nathaniel Mills, may cost several hundred pounds; indeed, a jewelled card case could cost thousands. But these are exceptional: more often, silver castle-top card cases fall into the £100–£200 bracket, depending on the reputation of the maker, the rarity of the subject and the condition of the case itself. The lack of hallmarks on American silver cases is generally reflected in much lower prices in comparison with English examples.

After silver, the more elaborate ivory, mother-of-pearl or tortoiseshell cases can cost as much as £75 or £100 if they are of outstanding quality, although the majority can be bought for between £20 and £40. Unusual cases are not always the most expensive: examples in leather, wood and materials like gun-metal, horn, and papier mâché may be found for well under £20 by the diligent searcher.

As with most collectors' items, it is

102. *(left)* This view of the Scott Memorial, made in the same year (1844) as that of fig. 101 (but by a slightly less celebrated silversmith, Joseph Taylor, of Birmingham), fetched £140 at Sotheby's in 1981.

103. *(right)* Another silver case by Nathaniel Mills, depicting The Temple of the Winds with Holyrood House in the background, Birmingham, 1845. This example fetched £140 in 1980.

important to buy what you like and buy the best you can afford. That does not mean buying the most expensive cases, but rather those that most effectively illustrate their type in whatever material. Look for fine workmanship, rare designs, unusual mechanisms or interior fittings, or uncommon materials. If a case particularly appeals to you, have the courage to buy it even if it seems a lot of money: you will not regret it.

Condition is very important. The first thing to look at, especially in tortoiseshell and mother-of-pearl cases, is the hinge and fastening. These are often damaged or broken, and the edges of the case around them may also be in disrepair. Look for missing fragments of veneer on wood, mother-of-pearl or tortoiseshell cases, chips or bruises on papier mâché and dents in metalwork. If a damaged case fills a gap in the collection and illustrates a rare type it should not be dismissed, but it is better to buy undamaged and, if possible, unrestored examples whenever possible.

Be careful to buy card cases if that is your intention: purses and pocket books, cigar and cheroot cases are often similar in shape and design. A little knowledge and careful examination will establish the difference. A wooden case with a silver foil lining for example, would have been intended for cigars or cheroots and not cards. Purses too are generally distinguishable by their interior fittings. In principle, be wary of any case with unusual proportions. Some card cases have been forced

104. *(left)* An unusual engraved terrace scene with a peacock in flight, two pot plants in the foreground and a fir tree and a willow. The back is engraved with a vase of flowers, and both are surrounded by scrolling foliage. It was made by Nathaniel Mills, Birmingham 1842, and fetched £130 at Phillips in 1979.

105. *(centre)* A Taylor & Perry silver case depicting Windsor Castle on one side and Kenilworth on the other, Birmingham 1842, which fetched £130 at Sotheby's. in 1981.

106. *(right)* A case engraved and engine-lined with a view of Windsor Castle surrounded by flowers and scrolls. Made in Birmingham in 1858 by Nathaniel Mills, and still complete with its original outer case, it fetched £150 at Phillips in 1979.

107. *(left)* A silver case made in Birmingham by Taylor & Perry in 1836 with a view of Abbotsford on this side and Newstead Abbey on the other. Its early date and the fact that it had views on both sides, as well as its excellent condition raised a price of £290 at Phillips in 1979.

108. *(right)* A sign of the times or a bargain? This case, by the same maker (Taylor & Perry) as fig. 107, depicting the same scenes (Newstead Abbey on this side and Abbotsford on the other) and dated a year earlier (1835) only fetched £100 at Sotheby's in 1981. It certainly serves as a reminder that prices for card cases, like all antiques, can fluctuate drastically.

up in the world: in the past, silver card case panels have occasionally been cut down and used for (more valuable) snuff box lids. Collectors of snuff boxes, more than card cases, should be awake to this reprehensible practice.

Repairs should, on the whole, be undertaken only by experts, but small chips of, for example, mother-of-pearl, tortoiseshell or wood veneers can usually be glued back in position without undue difficulty. An animal glue should be used mainly because synthetic

109. An elegantly simple mother-of-pearl card case of the type which can still be found in good condition for around £20.

110. Decorative effects such as these diamond shapes in contrasting shades may lift the price of a mother-of-pearl case into the £20–£30 bracket.

glues are permanent and irreversible. Silver card cases should be cleaned with a proprietary solution and polished with a soft cloth or brush (for embossed decoration). An important precept with regard to all silver is that no piece should be cleaned on a hard surface. Hold it in your hand or on your lap, and do not attack it with more than gentle pressure.

Mother-of-pearl can be cleaned by rubbing carefully with a swab of cotton wool dipped in a mild detergent solution and then squeezed well to ensure that no water gets into the cracks between the slices of shell. After cleaning, a gentle rub with wax polish will maintain the surface gloss.

Tortoiseshell on the other hand, should never be cleaned with detergent. Instead, rub the surface either with a finger or a soft cloth dipped in almond or olive oil, and then polish with the palm of the hand until all the oil has disappeared. Tortoiseshell and ivory piqué can also be effectively cleaned in this way. Papier mâché may be polished with a soft cloth and a light furniture oil, taking care not to catch any fragments of pearl shell that may have lifted. Finally, never leave your card cases in direct heat or sunlight: they can be permanently damaged by both.

It is always worth cataloguing a collection. A notebook recording details of purchases or gifts can provide a fascinating background. Write down when and where each case was purchased and how much you paid, as well as any historical details you may have been able to glean through dealers, auctioneers or your own researches.

Silversmiths known to have made card cases

The following silversmiths are among those known to have made card cases:

Birmingham makers	cases have been found between or around these dates
Nathaniel Mills	1833 – 1858
Taylor & Perry	1830 – 1842
George Unite	1859 – 1900
Edward Turpenny	1852
Hilliard & Thomason	1850 – 1879
Bettridge & Son	1850
Alfred Taylor	1853 – 1858
William Dudley	1850
Edward Smith	1841 – 1869
Joseph Willmore	1835 – 1844
Yapp & Woodward	1845 – 1853
David Pettifer	1850 – 1851
Elkington & Co.	1840s – 1880s
Thomas Prime & Sons	1888
Frederick Marson	1844 – 1860
Deakin & Francis	1894 – 1900
H. W. Dee } L. W. Dee }	1870s – 1890s

London Makers	
Sampson Mordan	1872 – 1907
Thomas Johnson	
Barnard Bros.	1880s

Chester, *Exeter* and *Dublin* marks have also been noted on card cases

Subjects found on Castle-top card cases

Abbotsford House
Albert Memorial
Anne Hathaway's Cottage
Battle Abbey
Birmingham Town Hall
Brighton Pavilion
Castle Howard
Chain Pier, Brighton
Crystal Palace
Exeter Cathedral
Houses of Parliament
Kenilworth Castle
King's College Chapel, Cambridge
Lanercost Abbey
Newstead Abbey
Nile 'Phile'
Osborne House
Royal Exchange
St. Paul's Cathedral
Scott Memorial
Scottish Castles: Borthwick, Melrose, Crichton and Lochleven
Temple of the Winds (and Holyrood House in the background)
Warwick Castle
Wellington Monument
Westminster Abbey
Windsor Castle

Books for Further Reading

Crisp-Jones, Kenneth *The Silversmiths of Birmingham and their Marks 1750–1980*, NAG Press, 1981.
Delieb, Eric *Silver Boxes*, Herbert Jenkins, 1968.
Hughes, Therle *Small Antiques for the Collector* Lutterworth, 1964.
Savage, George *Dictionary of 19th Century Antiques and Later Objets d'Art*, Barrie & Jenkins, 1978.
Spaulding de Voe, Shirley *English Papier Mâché of the Georgian and Victorian Periods*, Barrie & Jenkins, 1971.
Wildeblood, John *The Polite World*, Davis Poynter, 1973.

Acknowledgements

The author and publishers would like to thank the following for permission to use the photographs in this book:
Messrs. Bonhams 2, 3, 4, 5, 10, 12, 17, 18, 19, 20, 21, 31, 32, 33, 35, 36, 38, 39, 40, 41, 42, 49, 56, 57, 60, 60a, 61, 69, 70, 71, 72, 73, 74, 78, 79, 80, 81, 86, 91, 95, 96, 98, 99, 101, 103, 109; Harris Museum, Preston 28, 37, 45, 48, 52, 53, 54, 55, 62, 63, 64, 65, 66, 67, 68, 75, 76, 82, 83, 84, 85, 89, 90, 92, 93, 110; M. McAleer 6, 7, 11, 23, 29, 30, 50, 77, 100; Phillips Auctioneers 1, 8, 9, 15, 16, 24, 34, 104, 106, 107; Messrs. Sotheby's 13, 14, 22, 25, 26, 27, 102, 105, 108.

The author would also like to thank the following individuals for their help with this book: Eric Smith, Phillips; Ian Venture, Bonhams; Alex Walker, The Harris Museum, Preston; Yvonne Jones, Wolverhampton Art Gallery and Museums; Susan Hare, Goldsmiths Company; M. McAleer, London, W.1.

Index

Bold page numbers refer to illustrations